Sovereignty
of the Imagination

BOOKS BY HOUSE OF NEHESI PUBLISHERS

Guanahani, My Love
Marion Bethel

The Salt Reaper
Selected poems from the flats (Audio CD)
Lasana M. Sekou

Love Labor Liberation
IN LASANA SEKOU
Howard A. Fergus

Eva/Sión/Es • Eva/Sion/s • Éva/Sion/s
Chiqui Vicioso

Cul-de-Sac People - A St. Martin Family Series
Mathias S. Voges

The Angel Horn
Shake Keane (1927-1997) Collected Poems
Shake Keane

Salted Tongues
Modern Literature in St.Martin
Fabian Adekunle Badejo

Somebody Blew Up America & Other Poems
Amiri Baraka

The Essence of Reparations
Amiri Baraka

Friendly Anger
The Rise of the Labor Movement in St. Martin
Joseph H. Lake, Jr.

Words Need Love Too
Kamau Brathwaite

Coming, Coming Home - Conversations II
Western Education & The Caribbean Intellectual
George Lamming

Sovereignty of the Imagination

Conversations III

SOVEREIGNTY OF THE IMAGINATION
LANGUAGE AND THE POLITICS OF ETHNICITY

George Lamming

House of Nehesi Publishers
P.O. Box 460
Philipsburg, St. Martin
Caribbean

WWW.HOUSEOFNEHESIPUBLISH.COM

© 2009 George Lamming.

All rights reserved.
ISBN: 978-0-913441-46-6
LC Control Number: 2009923573

These new editions of "Sovereignty of the Imagination" and "Language and the Politics of Ethnicity" by Dr. George Lamming, are collected in this one volume for the first time as the third book in the *Conversations* series. Certain passages may be repeated in each essay. Versions of both essays have appeared singularly in book, journal, and Internet form and presented at distinguished lecture series between 2002 and 2007.

Cover, graphics design by Sundiata Lake
Cover art: "The Last Tree in Free Town" 2005, digital illustration by Angelo Rombley, © Angelo Rombley. Private collection.
Photography: Saltwater Collection

For Andaiye and Eusi Kwayana

Contents

Introduction	ix
1 Sovereignty of the Imagination	1
Contradictions	7
Political Parties and Trade Unionism	13
Eric Williams and a Concept of University	22
George Beckford: Utopian Realism	33
The Practice of Literature is Rooted in these Questions	36
Conclusion	44
Notes	48
Selected Bibliography	49
2 Language and the Politics of Ethnicity	51
Notes	80
Bibliography	81
About the Author	82

Introduction

When George Lamming rose to speak at the final session of the conference in his honor hosted by the Centre for Caribbean Thought,[1] he embodied many of our modern male ancestors. Here was a living link to C. L. R. James, Eric Williams, Martin Carter, Walter Rodney, Frantz Fanon, Edgar Mittelholzer, Alejo Carpentier, and Nicolás Guillén. The hushed tones in which the audience received his speech of over two hours was in part the manner of its delivery—a manner in which, in cricketing parlance, a crowd absorbs and relishes an exquisite stroke play while on the pitch: "not a man move." But there was another reason for the hushed tones. Lamming was speaking against the backdrop of a pervading Caribbean sense that across the region, the independence anticolonial projects had floundered and spun off into different directions ... directions that oftentimes ran counter to the vast expectations of the ordinary Caribbean person. So here was an individual who began to write novels about the Caribbean in its final phases of formal constitutional decolonization, who had grown up under a colonial empire; here he was now speaking from a past, but in a language that beckoned us to a different future. We were not watching the performance of orality, as his distinctive voice and clear Caribbean cadences moved through the audience. We were hushed because we knew that many of the ancestors' memories were being invoked.

The reader of this document will make her or his own

decision about the critical points of this seminal speech. However, we know that the power of speech is different from that of voice. It is speech and language that allow us to construct our reflections and experiences of the world. George Lamming has always been preoccupied with two things: the character of what our language constructs and the ways in which these constructions foreclose freedom. It is why, for Lamming, speaking is so important. He says, "(A speech) does not work like a novel. It is a very different kind of language. The speeches are addressed to the mind. ... The speeches are given in what we would call a language of statements. But statement given and structured in such a way that makes the mind feel."[2]

In his 1956 speech to what is conventionally referenced as the First International Congress of Black Writers and Artists in Paris, and four years after the publication of Frantz Fanon's *Black Skin, White Masks*, Lamming draws our attention with the following statement: "For it is one of the mischievous powers of language, and particularly that aspect of language which relates to names.... Language in this respect is intentional, and the intention seems clearly part of the human will to power. A name is an infinite source of control."[3]

For Lamming, the power to name is not only a power to define, but also, more importantly, it opens the power to understand the Caribbean self and its social and historical realities within the Caribbean's own frames. In his 1960 novel *Season of Adventure*, the character Baako proclaims, "... the main problem was language.... But remember the order of the drums, he finished, for it is the language which every nation needs if its promises and its myths are to become a fact."[4] The *Sovereignty of the Imagination* gives us that capacity for language and therefore the ability to name and establish categories. But this is not just a literary capacity; it allows us to define freedom. George Lamming recognizes the centrality of the quest for freedom for the social group that he calls "this world of men and women from down below." Again, referring to *Season of Adventure*, we read the following dialogue about freedom between two of the novel's central figures, Powell and Crim. Powell says, "Independence aint nothin' till it free...." He continues, "Free is how you is from the start,... an' when you movin' say that is a natural freedom make you move. You can't move to freedom, Crim, 'cause freedom is what you is, an' where you start, an' where you always got to stand." The dialogue represents both a deeply moving and profound enunciation of the human condition. It posits how the anticolonial struggle morphed into the denial of human freedom, how political independence of the postcolony became limited and expectant hopes dashed. The tight relationship between politics, knowledge, language, and the spaces of freedom in Lamming's writings makes him one of the most important political novelists in Caribbean literature; one who also understands that the brutal histories of slavery and colonialism did not crush nor erase creativity.

Lamming's preoccupation with freedom is today very apropos because one feature of our contemporary world is the resurgence of a current of thought and action, which heralds the virtues of empire. Empire, today sometimes called by its advocates liberal imperialism, announces to the world that the real meanings of freedom are to be found in the values, creeds, and myths of those who are powerful and have dominated the world for the last five hundred years. These so-called virtues of empire proclaim the end of history and hope to suck all humanity into its vortex. For George Lamming, one terror of the old colonial empire was what he calls "the terror of the mind," a peculiar toxic form of hegemony that seeks to shape and bend the subject it rules. In the present world, the dominant hegemony hopes to bend us to its will and shape our very desires. In such a context, the sovereignty of the imagination becomes one foundation for the imagining and desire for freedom. Lamming notes in a timely interview, "Freedom is where you are and where you start.... That is your original spiritual oxygen.... And the struggle is to discover it and to discover its potential and to discover the ways in which potential can be made to exercise itself in a variety of ways...."[5]

What George Lamming beckons us toward is the constructive use of this potential in building Caribbean society.

> Anthony Bogues
> Professor of Africana Studies and
> Political Science, Brown University

Notes

[1] George Lamming addressed the final session of the conference in his honor, hosted by the Centre for Caribbean Thought, University of the West Indies, Jamaica, 2003.

[2] Andaiye, Forward - "The Public Task of George Lamming's Caribbean Speeches," *Conversations: George Lamming Essays, Addresses and Interviews 1953-1990*, Richard Drayton and Andaiye, eds. (London: Karia Press, 1992) 7.

[3] George Lamming, "The Negro Writer and his World," *Conversations: George Lamming Essays, Addresses and Interviews 1953-1990*, Richard Drayton and Andaiye, eds. (London: Karia Press, 1992) 38.

[4] George Lamming, *Season of Adventure* (Ann Arbor: The University of Michigan Press, 1999) 363.

[5] David Scott, "The Sovereignty of the Imagination: An Interview with George Lamming," *Small Axe* 12 (2002) 146.

✿ ✿ ✿

1
SOVEREIGNTY OF THE IMAGINATION[1]

At the historic trial of Fidel Castro after the unsuccessful raid on Moncada, Castro, a lawyer by training, rested his defense on the spiritual guidance of José Martí. "We are proud of the history of our country," he told the judges. "We learned it in school. Céspedes, Maceo, Gomez, and Martí were the first names engraved in our minds. We were taught that for the guidance of Cuba's free citizens." The Apostle Martí wrote, "In the world there must be a certain degree of honor just as there must be a certain amount of light. When there are many men without honor, there are always others who bear in themselves the honor of many men...."

Addressing the Eighth Convocation Ceremony of the University of Guyana in 1974, Martin Carter said, "It is precisely in times of crisis that we must re-examine our lives and bring to that re-examination contempt for the trivial, and respect of the riskers—those who take the risk of going forward boldly to participate in the building of a free community of valid persons...."

These are two texts I ask you to consider and, alongside them, the concept of honor and the free community of valid persons.

I was the child of a fundamentalist Christian home, which literally believed and lived by the precepts of the Sermon on the Mount. We were among the poor, the merciful, the meek, the peacemakers. Survival in the most adverse conditions had certainly made us, in some way, the salt of the earth; and I was persuaded by an ambitious mother that I would, by some miracle, become a light that would shine before men. There is some argument about this prediction, but my presence here may be some consolation that there has been illumination of some kind. The negative aspect of this legacy was just as powerful. Sin was not a word whose meanings invited argument. It was a kind of barometer that measured a great variety of activity or intended action, which it was with me. I always suspect the means whereby the rich accumulate their wealth, and I am inclined to agree with Balzac that every great fortune begins with a crime.

My home forbade any form of betting, and although I have a great curiosity about the psychology of gamblers, I have retained to this day a strange, emotional block about gambling. There was, in the early Christianity of that house, a moral force that enabled me to see much later what was essentially right about the social thought of socialist philosophy: the poor as the key for change; the oppressed and exploited as the ultimate inheritors of the earth;

the present as a battleground for the possessions of the future. Christians and socialists are inseparable on this emphasis on the human expectations of the earth. But Christianity never provided me with a critique of my relation to where I was born or the social forces shaping my beliefs. My early education in Barbados was a total product of Christian indoctrination. I use the terms total and indoctrination because no one in the role of teacher had ever drawn our attention to the historical truth that Christianity was only one of several great religions, or that Christians then, as they do now, represented a minority of the world's population.

The fictional account in *In the Castle of My Skin* of boys' speculation on slavery and the Garden of Eden may be a pretty accurate reflection of what was a genuine, popular belief among the poor at the time:

> The queen freed some of us because she made us feel the empire was bigger than the garden. That's what the old woman meant. The queen did free some of us in a kind of way. We started to think about the empire more than we thought of the garden, and then nothing mattered but the empire. But they have put the two of them together now. The empire and garden. We are to speak of them the same way. They belong to the same person. They both belong to God. The garden is God's own garden and the empire is God's only empire.

The entire globe was the spiritual property of the Christian God. This religious proposition was supported by a secular doctrine that presented the British Empire as the political custodian of all human destiny. We were made aware of rival powers—French and German perhaps—but these did not exist as human entities in their own right. They were interlopers who represented a heretical challenge to what had been divinely ordained as the limits of human reality: the Christian God, as creator of the universe, and the British Empire, as His temporal trustee.

In this respect, it is not an exaggeration to say that both church and school were agents of an intellectual and moral deception. I would not argue that it was their conscious intention to play this role; it is more likely that they were functioning as institutions that had been conditioned to reflect and support the prevailing values and demands of those who ruled the society. The religious functionary, irrespective of denomination, became associated in my mind as being an accomplice in the support and preservation of the existing *status quo*. And in Barbados that meant racism, economic exploitation, and a profound contempt for all that was black. Even among its ranks, the Church refused to disturb this social arrangement and found a sacred text to approve its conduct. Paul writing to the Romans (13:1-2), notes, "Let every person be subject to the governing authorities, for there is no authority except God, and those that exist have been instituted by God. Therefore, he who resists the authorities resists what God has appointed."

This cultural conviction can become toxic as you move from origins to unknown territory, territory you assumed you had known. In 1950 when I went to England, migration was not a word I would have used to describe what I was doing. We simply thought that we were going to an England that had been planted in our childhood consciousness as a heritage and a place of welcome. It is the measure of our innocence that neither the claim of heritage nor the expectation of welcome would have been seriously doubted. England was not, for us, a country with classes and conflicts of interest like the island we had left. It was the name of a responsibility whose origin may have coincided with the beginning of time. This has happened elsewhere in peculiar ways; in Sierra Leone a colleague of mine asked a sixteen-year-old student: "What do you think the letters BBC stand for?" And she replied, "Before the birth of Christ?"

Later I would shudder to think how a country so foreign to our instincts could have achieved the miracle of being called mother. It has made us pupils to its language, its institutions; baptized us in the same religion; schooled boys in the same game of cricket with its elaborate and meticulous etiquette of rivalry. Empire was not a very dirty word, and seemed to bear little relation to those forms of domination we call imperialist. The English themselves were not aware of the role they had played in the formation of these black strangers. The ruling class was serenely confident that any role of theirs must have been an act of supreme generosity, and like Prospero, they had given us language and a way of naming our own reality. But the English working class was not aware they had played any role at all, and deeply resented our arrival. It had come about without any warning; no one had consulted them. Occasionally I was asked, "Do you belong to us, or to the French?" I had been dissolved in the common view of worker and aristocrat. So even English workers could see themselves as architects of Empire.

Much of the substance of *In the Castle of My Skin* is an evocation of this tragic innocence. Nor was there at the time of writing any conscious effort on my part to emphasize the dimension of cruelty which had seduced, or had driven by force of need, an otherwise honorable black people into such lasting bonds of illusion, such toxic forms of cultural conviction. For it was not a physical cruelty that we knew. Indeed, the colonial experience of my generation was almost wholly without violence—no torture, no concentration camp, no mysterious disappearance of hostile natives, no army encamped with orders to kill. The Caribbean endured a different kind of subjugation: it was *a terror of the mind*, a daily exercise in self-mutilation, black versus black in a battle for self-improvement. This was the breeding ground for every uncertain self. But there was one area of ground where certainty had taken the form of the legend.

Contradictions

Now, I grew up as a boy with the legend that the greatest batsman in the world was George Headley—and there is some part of me that still believes that the greatest batsman in the world was George Headley—but I have never seen Headley bat. I have read about Headley, who nearly always made half the score on good wickets and bad wickets. And so when I returned to the Caribbean from England, stopping at Jamaica, I had a friend who was very close to Headley—the novelist Neville Dawes—and I told him that one of my greatest ambitions would be to meet Headley. And he took me to meet Headley—a very small, very elegant, and very gracious man. And I was asking him the sorts of questions that novices ask: I wanted to know whether the fast bowlers like Martindale and Francis were faster than Hall and Griffith and such people, and so on. It was very interesting—he never replied to the question in that way. He replied by saying what he thought was the difference between them, but he never got involved in who was faster or who was better.

But I refer to him also because he mentioned the name Herman Griffith, and he mentioned the name Herman Griffith with great respect. Now, you will realize that in the twenties and thirties there would have been great tension around race and color in the West Indies cricket team. And Headley said that he was struck by the dignity of Griffith, while others would whisper and complain; if there was ever an occasion of racial insult, he remembered Griffith not only for his tactical skills (he was a great bowler); he remembered him always for the extraordinary pride he had in the value of his skin and in the dignity of his person. Here I offer an example of the contradictions in certain political crusades.

Now, when I was about to leave Combermere, they had a tradition where you might become a schoolboy member of one of the leading clubs, and I was spotted and invited to join Empire. So I played a few games for Empire before leaving for Trinidad. There was a regulation that as a schoolboy member you did not pay any subs for a year. And one Saturday afternoon we were playing Wanderers (I remember it very well); I was fielding at cover point.

Harold Griffith, the son of Herman Griffith, was bowling; and then Herman Griffith walked onto the field while Harold Griffith was running up, and he was walking toward me. Harold Griffith stopped and came over to find out what had happened, and it turned out that Herman Griffith had come to ask me about the subs. This is 2 o'clock in the afternoon, on Empire grounds, with an enormous crowd. Herman Griffith had come to remind me that the subs had not been paid, and the eighteen months had passed. Harold told him that he had to leave the field because it could not be discussed at that time. I was very struck, thinking back on this—how the man Headley described and the man for whom I had the greatest admiration as I got to know him—how this man could have also created a record of having blackballed more people than probably all the clubs in Barbados. He was an emperor of Empire, and you could not get into Empire if you had not gone at least to Combermere. You only have to think of the enormous giants of West Indies cricket who would not have made it into Empire: Weekes, Sobers, Haynes, Charlie Griffith.

And that is what I mean by our fundamental contradiction in every political crusade: on one hand, this audacious representative of a race, and on the other, the total insensitivity to the hurt, the pain, the alienation of causing social rejection. These two attributes lived side by side in the one man. The contradiction is to be found in a variety of citizens across the region.

This region has been staggering slowly and painfully to resolve the contradiction of being at once independent and neocolonial; struggling through new definitions of itself to abandon the protection of being a frontier created by nature, a logistical basin serving some imperial necessity; and struggling to move away from being a regional platform for alien enterprise to the status of being a region for itself, with the sovereign right to define its own reality and order its own priorities.

Ordinary people continue to devise their own strategies for contact and communication, through a network of petty trading that links Jamaica and Haiti, Barbados and St. Lucia, Grenada and Trinidad, Dominica and St. Martin, defying the constraints which are imposed by the region's highest councils of government, immigration laws, work permits, and the opportunistic hassle about who is and who is not a national from one territory to the next. And yet it is argued everywhere that these people are the critical motive force of the society. But it is a force which has too often been reduced to the dormant and abused status of electoral fodder. Every four or five years, they become visible and decisive in a tribal power game that concludes with their absence from any serious consultation about their future. It is a predicament of which Mr. Owen Arthur, the prime minister of Barbados, must have been very aware because in September 1999, he made the most extraordinary statement in Jamaica relating directly to this kind of situation:

> To realize its full potential, the Caribbean needs to move to a new form of governance. No Caribbean society can succeed unless all of its resources are mobilized into support of national development. However, the unfortunate aspect of the Westminster model of governance we have inherited is that it has encouraged a 'to the victors, the spoils' mentality. And that has ensured that at any time, almost half the population of any given Caribbean society is marginalized and alienated from participation in the development of their society. There has been too destructive a competition for political office, too heavy a concentration of power in the hands of ruling elites, an unhealthy preservation of anti-developmental party and tribal divisions, a focus on short-term partisan political concerns, and a patronage spoils system which works against sound and progressive government.

Mr. Arthur is in fact seriously questioning the dysfunctional nature of the existing political system.

And more than 50 years before, we hear Norman

Manley of Jamaica say:

> The mass of the population are the real people. Those who would not unite with them in all fundamental matters are the real aliens in the land. And we believe that the people must believe in themselves and their own destiny and must do so with pride and with confidence and with determination to win equality with the rest of mankind, an equality in terms of humanity which, irrespective of power and wealth, can be measured by the growing values of civilization and culture.

It has been more than half a century since Norman Manley made this statement. It was part of a wider plea for greater civic responsibility among the privileged classes and in public life. During that interval, we have seen the emergence of new class formations and the elevation of black people to high office and more elaborate styles of material comfort. But it does not appear that this change in fortune has made any substantial difference in the relationship between leadership and those who are led. The temptation to find the shortest route possible to wealth has increased. And so has the frustration of an idle and disenchanted youth. The rural population continues its decline; the cities grow more crowded and more dangerous. From Kingston to Port of Spain, the story is much the same. And immigration is a rescue that is only available to those who have had expensive training and whose skills ensure their survival elsewhere.

Political Parties and Trade Unionism

Now, in Caribbean history, as you know, the political party and the trade union movement have had a simultaneous birth—twin institutions that grew out of the same struggle of the 1930s. But there was already some element of distortion in this composition of party and trade union. The impulse to break out of colonial rule did not guarantee the necessary break away from colonial tutelage. These institutions, party and union, were native—a genuine creation of people's power—but their leadership retained a special loyalty to the old imperial guidelines. The Barbadian Mr. Lawrence Nurse has written very perceptively on this. In an essay titled "Organised Labour in the Caribbean Commonwealth," he says:

> The 1930s represented an effective challenge which brought together sectional interests: proletariat, peasants, and members of an emergent middle-class. The proletariat and the peasants entered the struggle in protest against the social economic deprivation: the middle-class, though arguing for the franchise and right of political rights, was interested in political power for itself. Organised labour became the major force in the democratization of Caribbean societies. They challenged the insult of racial discrimination which retarded the progress

of the black middle-class. They fought for the extension of the franchise until universal adult suffrage was achieved. They secured the legal rights of the trade union in a series of constitutional reforms, which led ultimately to political independence.

"But," continues Nurse, "all these forces served well the political interest of the middle-class. Political leaders gave their approval to a particular type of union, and institutionalized the Westminster two-party model of government in the region."

And so, what started as a radical response to the planter oligarchy of the day was gradually led into a series of compromises, which now make the victory of the 1930s seem less secure. Rex Nettleford, the vice chancellor of the University of the West Indies, is a very prudent man; when reflecting on nation-building, he expresses this apprehension: "I have a deep concern that trade unions are being pushed further and further on the periphery of all social and economic arrangements throughout the Caribbean region, for the convenience of the historical plantocracy, the enduring commission agency class, and the newly-arrived technocracy."

The last 60 years since 1938 must be regarded, therefore, as a period of transition. We have seen the gradual erosion of an old social order: the political directorates have changed complexion, but they operate within the same basic institutions. There has been no great structural change in the patterns of ownership and control. And the new political directorates have never been a part of the old ruling planter and merchant class. They govern, but they do not rule. The transnational corporation assumed a novel dominance in all regional affairs. Domestic policy is determined by international lending agencies. Independence has not yet won the right to sovereignty.

If we go back to 1965, one of our greatest historians, Professor Elsa Goveia, in her most extraordinary book *Slave Society in the British Leeward Islands at the end of the eighteenth century*, gave this warning:

> Ever since the time of emancipation ... we have been trying to combine opposite principles in our social system, but sooner or later we shall have to face the fact that we are courting defeat when we attempt to build a new heritage of freedom upon a structure of society which binds us all too closely to the old heritage of slavery. Liberty and equality are good consorts, for though their claims sometimes conflict, they rest upon a common basis which makes them reconcilable. But the most profound incompatibility necessarily results from the uneasy union which joins democracy with the accumulated remains of enslavement.

We've had three alternative experiments to what Mr. Arthur was talking about, and each offers a lesson in failure. Grenada was both a heroic and tragic suicidal experience. During its brief period of four years, the Maurice Bishop administration provided an example of genuine commitment to change and had made much progress in creating institutions that would ensure effective people's participation in self-management, or so it seemed. It was the only experiment of the three that had captured the imagination of the country's youth. Guyana emerges as the least worthy of respect. It is here the word "socialist" was reduced to the language of blasphemy and lost its power to inspire. On the other hand, Michael Manley never enjoyed the power and control which Bishop and Forbes Burnham, in different ways, had appropriated. Manley was in fact the victim of external pressure in the form of national sabotage, which was the weapon the privileged classes of Jamaica used against his administration. But his failure must also be attributed to a serious lack of preparation.

The experiment to place the mass of the population in a new and critical relation to power came up against a certain lack of comprehension on the part of those who were to benefit from the change. Writing in 1984 in "Aspects of a Caribbean Development Strategy," Manley concedes this weakness, which was a critical factor in his loss of power:

It is now clear that as part of the political organisation's response, political education in a profound sense has got to be the heart and stock of the political process. This political education begins by a process of internal educational dialogue; it looks at the social and political history that begins with simple, basic analysis of the nature of the society, the nature of the economy, the nature of its class structure.

And I want to say that as far as I am aware, no political party in the Commonwealth Caribbean has ever shown much enthusiasm for carrying out, in a systematic way, the kind of program of political education that Manley acknowledges to be essential to any major change in popular consciousness.

For over half a century, the leadership of both party and union, from territory to territory, has deliberately omitted this basic work from their programs of mass organization. The omission could not have been casual; and we must assume that many a leader, then and now, recognized that such political education at mass level would inevitably alter the relation of leader to rank and file. It would have required putting an end to the uncritical adoration of the leader as great tribal chief, infallible beyond reproach. For this has been a characteristic deformity of the political culture of the region, and it has persisted, whatever the ideological character of the leader.

The late Carl Stone, a social scientist, has made reference to this tendency to personalize power at the expense of institutional machinery. He goes further in identifying the cause of failure in these experiments in socialist transformation:

> In all three cases, efforts of transformation centred on political structures and the character of political power without sufficient attention to spelling out and articulating the new society and the new Caribbean man that would have been the fundamental objective of the exercise, as well as the vehicle for achieving its objectives.

Political strategies and objectives toward socialist change were often clearly articulated, but there was, I quote again, "no commanding vision of the new society to be created." This is, I think, a just evaluation of the limitations at work among political activists at the time; but it assumes too much, and it stops short of being a comprehensive critique of the society. For we should never assume that the political man is always suitably equipped to articulate a commanding vision of a new society. The politician is overwhelmed by concrete tasks to be performed, decisions to be taken urgently, often without any pause for long reflection. He or she is haunted by the failure to deliver. Their working hours are spent in a permanent state of emergency. The shadow of parliamentary opposition, where it exists, blurs their sense of priorities. They live with intrigue and the constant threat of betrayal within their own ranks. It is, I suspect, a feverish atmosphere and hardly conducive to that state of reflective self-consciousness from which a vision of new society is born.

But it is possible that the political leader could not arrive at such a vision unless he enjoyed a certain measure of collaborative support from other modes of thought and perception, from the historian, the poet, the student of philosophy and the social sciences, the economist, and the theater director who recreates the cultural history of the nation. It is a collective dialogue between these different categories of sensibility which ultimately gives voice to a commanding vision of the new society. But it is precisely this voice which has often withdrawn its service from any form of political engagement. There is a large category of intellectual workers who view such involvement with misgivings. The risks are too great.

A novelist sets out to explore the history and the nature of an individual or personal relationship. But every personal relationship is a social fact because the relationship is engaged with another, and is influenced by the others who may or may not be directly connected to the individuals. Boy meets girl, there is parent involvement, friend involvement. Boy seeks employment, may require medical report from a doctor he's never seen before, and so on. All our relations are experienced within a particular context of power, and it is the characteristic of all power that it seeks to give its existence some moral or philosophical justification.

Men do not simply say, "We are in power because we feel we have a right to be and that's the end of that. There's nothing you can do about it." They never say that. They believe they represent and are the guardians of some social order, which is in the interest of all, and then they will hire a variety of intellectual mercenaries to argue that this is true. This social order is usually supportive of the material interest of the dominant ruling group, and they translate these interests as being identical with the interest of the total society. But many other layers of the society recognize, through their own daily experience, that there is no such identity of interest. To assert this fact of their experience is to pose a conflict of contending interests. In other words, class—that is, categories of persons who are conscious of interests that are in opposition to the interests of other categories of persons—to one degree or another, is an informing influence on the imagination of every serious writer who tries to record and interpret the content of an individual relationship.

Or to put it another way, a concept of people and places does not arise out of the blue. How you come to think of where you are, and how you come to think of your relation to where you are, is very dependent on what is the character and the nature of power, where you are. You yourself do not at a certain stage decide who you are, and what your relationship to where you are should be. These relations are experienced within a specific context of power, and this experience within a specific context poses always a fundamental question: to what extent have we been able to organize in the interest of our own welfare? To what extent can we/have we been able to organize in the interest of our lives? Economists will frequently identify the problems of scarcity, which justify their own professional expertise. Scarcity may be due to natural calamity, or scarcity may be manufactured. But the economists are reluctant to explore and reveal the nature of the exercise of the power which determines these things. If we are trying to think of concepts of islands and region, these concepts will undergo a certain change; they will differ according to the centers of power that are shaping them, according to the centers of resistance to that power.

Hegemony is the domination of one class over another or all others, and not necessarily through force but through a process of social, political, and ideological indoctrination in order to achieve the consent of the dominated class. The dominant class will sometimes make concessions to the dominated, provided the long-term interests of the dominant group are not challenged or undermined. Its effect on the executive branch of the state and on civil society is considerable. And in civil society, we group organizations such as the Boy Scouts, Lions, Lionesses, charity organizations, and non-governmental organizations (NGOs). The consensus in Barbados on the discourse on race (not to raise it) is the influence of that hegemonic power. A variety of reasons are given: it could wreck the tourist industry and damage the economy of the nation; there is no place in a Christian society for race talk because all are equal in the sight of God. Therein the appeal to social stability and with the warning: Look at Trinidad! Look at Guyana!

Eric Williams and a Concept of University

In 1944 the British government announced the appointment of a commission to consider the needs of higher education in the colonies. You will note that we are just one year away from the end of Europe's second Civil War in the 20th century. I shall return a little later to the critical importance of those 31 years from 1914 to 1945, when European civilization committed itself to the slaughter of 187 million people.

It is at this critical juncture when new definitions will have to be found to clarify the meaning of the word "civilization" that the meetings to consider the creation of the University of the West Indies took place. The chairman was Sir John Irvine of St. Andrew's University, and it would appear from his own autobiographical account that Dr. Williams, then a professor of political science at Howard University, requested an opportunity to give evidence before the commission, which included Margery Perham of Oxford; Raymond Priestly of Birmingham; and from the Caribbean, the late Hugh Springer and Philip Sherlock. They met with Williams on May 29, 1944. It was not a very cordial encounter, but, more important for us, it was the genesis of what would become a seminal document now known as "Education of the Negro in the British West Indies." In this document, Williams outlines in great detail his conception of the kind of university that would be required for the Caribbean people at that stage of their subjugation—in the sense of restricted knowledge.

Williams's central theme, articulated in a variety of ways, is stated in one sentence of startling lucidity:

> Education in the modern world is, more than anything else, education of the people themselves as to the necessity of viewing their own education as a part of their democratic privileges and their demo-

cratic responsibilities.

And he will return again and again to this fundamental requirement that "from the very beginning the British West Indian masses should be educated as to the importance and necessity of the university; and through their popular and labour organisations, all should be made to feel that the university is an integral part of their own development...."

This was not a battle cry on behalf of masses, but his own historical training had left him with the conviction that the university, now known as the UWI, should be regional in character:

> The British West Indian University should, therefore, be a centre of culture of the entire Caribbean area, from Cuba to the Guianas. Regionalism should be its slogan; and the university should make it one of its various trends which have contributed to form the individual culture of the Caribbean.

He envisaged the early stages of the curriculum as a concentration on the social and economic needs of the islands, their geographical location, and the chief fields of employment available to graduates: agriculture, teaching, social work, public service, nursing, and sanitation. And always in the formulation of stages of curriculum, he would return to what seems to have struck him as a moral imperative: "The needs of the British West Indian masses," he writes, "should dictate the content of university education. Only to that degree is a modern university modern...." We are hearing here—though some 30 years earlier—the radical voice and accent of George Beckford and Walter Rodney.

This emphasis on the category we call masses, in whom the potential for creative intellectual development is never in doubt, is always linked to the regional obligations that should influence curriculum: "A general course in West Indian culture should be obligatory for all students in the freshman year, a broad course in West Indian agriculture, and two years of study of at least one language, and in French and Spanish civilization."

What he saw so clearly as urgent—and still from my observation remains a remote and vaguely desirable acquisition—was the need to promote and encourage a multilingual facility, which would be essential for any serious comparative study of what we now call a Caribbean civilization. Pressed for space, I once offered to give my old copies of the Puerto Rican journal *Claridad* to a lecturer at the Institute of Social and Economic Research at Cave Hill. He breezily informed me, "I don't read Spanish, and I don't know anybody around me who does...." There was no trace of regret in this claim to ignorance.

Williams had an incurable passion for all kinds of statistical detail, and he carried on (as his adversaries might say) about matters like the Jamaican diet and how many gallons of milk and how many eggs per person per annum made up the Jamaican diet.

These meetings of Williams and the Irvine commission could be interpreted as a genuine clash of principles between a convert and his original mentors. Remember, Williams was a double First Oxford product, and Howard was a long way from what Sir John Irvine would have thought he would want UWI to be. Williams understood this very well and took maximum advantage of the privilege of those who, once categorized as objects of study, become the historical subjects who will redefine the terrain that is up for study.

If the curriculum requirements posed awkward questions, these were nothing compared to the turbulence created by his insistence that the university should be located in the heart of Kingston, the capital of Jamaica. I want to offer the full passage of his report because students of Williams's career will recognize these affirmations of 1945 as a preparation of the voice which will, some 12 years later, create the most extraordinary people's intellectual environment in what would become known as the "University of Woodford Square":

This unitary university should be located in Kingston, the capital of Jamaica. There are those who argue that the needs of future expansion require that the university be located in the suburbs. But a modern university cannot be detached from the centre of community life; it must be established in the city proper. The sheltered groves in which the students of Plato and Aristotle walked and discussed were admirably suited to the education of a leisured class. The medieval cloisters on the banks of the Isis were well adapted to the training of the British aristocracy. A university in the modern world, however, is a part of the endowment of a great city. If London, Columbia, New York, and Chicago universities can find room for expansion, the overcrowding in Kingston need occasion no alarm. Such a university, located in Kingston, will become the centre for the intellectual youth of the area. It would be a concrete step in the direction of integration.

The committee was not very impressed. The late Sir Hugh questioned the prudence of a university in the heart of Kingston and asked with characteristic anxiety: "What will become of our daughters?" Well, I don't know what became of the daughters of Mona. But when I was writer-in-residence at UWI-Mona in 1967, I was approached by a very irate male student to intervene in rebuking the Warden of Seacole who had given permission for the ladies of Seacole to visit a German ship which was on some patrol in the Caribbean ... "Seacole ladies exposing themselves to German sailors until one and two in the morning!" He was absolutely scandalized..., and I was not unaffected since Seacole, exclusively female, had always been represented to me as "the impregnable fortress of the campus upper-class virgins." To escape, I asked what he thought would be the reaction if the German sailors were female, and the gentlemen of Chancellor had been invited as their guests.

It isn't Springer or the German ship that should detain us here, but the more formidable Sir John Irvine, the chairman of the commission. Williams thought that Irvine disliked him, and he reciprocated the feeling. But Irvine had maneuvered him into a private chat, and this is how, in Dr. Williams's version, it went:

Irvine: You are a West Indian, aren't you?
Williams: Yes.
Irvine: You would like to see the status of the West Indies improved, wouldn't you?
Williams: Yes.
Irvine: You agree therefore that the West Indies must have a university, don't you?
Williams: Yes.
Irvine: You agree that it must be a good university, don't you?
Williams: Yes.

Irvine: Therefore, you agree that that West Indian university must be affiliated to a British university, don't you?
Williams: No. Definitely not....

He requested Irvine's permission to submit a formal memorandum giving in detail his conception of a university. And once this was granted, Williams then sought an interview with the formidable American philosopher John Dewey, who was now in his eighties and alert as ever on matters pertaining to educational theory. Williams then went about excavating the literature of every commission and committee on education that had ever met between 1900 and 1940, and hit upon a statement by Lord Haldane who was head of the Royal Commission on university education in London in 1913. Lord Haldane was advising London University to abandon once and for all the pernicious theory underlying its present practice that the kind of education it thinks best for its own students must be the best for all people who owe allegiance to the British flag. Long after the flags have changed, the psychic allegiance has remained a formidable obstacle to the liberation of the intellect. How else can we explain the melancholy nostalgia for the British Privy Council as the final court of appeal; the spineless rejection of a Caribbean Court; or the excessive caution that restrains Barbados from converting its allegiance from the archaic ornamentalism of monarchy to republican status though the country is, according to Professor McKintosh, already a republic in social and political practice?

McKintosh's approach has a philosophical dimension which for him, as a professor of jurisprudence, becomes a moral imperative:

> With independence we acquired the authority to define ourselves as a community. The hope is that with a Caribbean Court of Appeal, we would be forced to construct our discourse, to reshape our world, much in line with what our poets and novelists have already begun. A Caribbean court of final appeal must be the centre of any discursive advancement toward the development of a Caribbean jurisprudence....
>
> Constitutional adjudication is a fundamental conceptual debate about the way in which Caribbean political life is to be constituted, lived, and justified ... and such an important matter should not be left in the hands of a British institution.

Which brings us to the astounding question posed by Sir Arthur Lewis and relates to the death of the Federation. Young men and women of my generation, nurtured on a strong regional orientation, were shattered by these events. I don't know if those of you born after the Independence settlements of the 1960s can quite understand this. But it was as though we had built a coffin for ourselves and were just waiting for whoever would come to negotiate the price of burial.

Lewis's question was brought to my attention by an article of Tim Hector's in a special Tim Hector issue of the *C.L.R. James Journal* (Vol. 8, No. 1). Lewis identifies the three major figures of that moment and begins by elaborating on their qualities:

> This is in itself odd since the three heads of government whose head-on collisions, despite their unquestioned allegiance to the cause, ultimately wrecked the Federation. Adams, Manley, and Williams were all men of the highest quality on any definition of the word. Their talents were outstanding and their education the envy of mankind.
>
> They were men of immaculate integrity and selfless devotion to the public service. Each was at the top of his profession before entering public life, and gained neither prestige nor money from entering politics. Each would be recognized in any country in the world as a public servant of highest caliber....

The question of questions posed by Sir Arthur was this: "How did these highly intelligent men, all devoted to Federation, come to make so many errors in so short a period? Clearly the leadership of the Federation was awful."

Lewis's judgment carries weight, but it is possible

that although he saw with great clarity the situation he describes and laments, he may have been looking in the wrong direction. The answer to his question, or some portion of that answer, may be found in the cultural displacement of the men involved. They were the brilliant products of an epistemological formation, which was in profound discord with the concrete and novel realities that now challenged the imagination. They were the casualties of an inherited tutelage, colonial in essence and thereby placed an overwhelming constraint on the concept of liberation. It had happened before and has been articulated with unsparing candor by the Argentinian thinker Ezequiel Estrada with reference to the crisis in leadership of Latin American liberation struggles that had in great agony won their release from the political domination of a colonizing European power:

> Neither here nor elsewhere is there any public awareness of the fact that cultural emancipation is not any easier although it may be less bloody than political liberty; and a great part of the failure of our independence movements was due to the fact that our liberators were not liberated from themselves. Mentally free, they were subconsciously in chains because they continued to accept the structure of European cultures, changing only their forms and a small part of their content, in the same way they had done with their political institutions.

George Beckford: Utopian Realism

George Beckford, who symbolized a point of preparation for transcendence, had this extraordinary conviction derived from acute observation and the sovereignty of the imagination that there existed in each territory, and the region as a whole, the capacity to provide for the basic needs of its population; that there was no objective reason why any citizen in Jamaica should go to bed hungry. The strategy of this achievement he called self-reliance, which could meet the society's basic needs of food, shelter, clothing, health, and education. But the major hurdle to the achievement of self-reliance was the question of consumer tastes. That was 1984. And what seemed a hurdle then has matured and gangrened into an irreversible delirium of consumption.

Let us pause and recall for a moment the positive side of his contention. G. Beck had just come back from the Far East and was struck by the fact that they were using bamboo for scaffolding in building construction. And suddenly he begins to think of Flat Bridge, which now reveals itself as a miracle: the Flat Bridge crosses the Rio Cobre River. This bridge was built before the days of concrete and steel. And every time that river comes down and overflows the road, we find that when the water subsides, Flat Bridge is still standing there. There is something remarkable about that bridge, but none of the structural engineers at the time seemed to know what binding material was in it. They only said that the thing was so beautifully designed. "It is our ancestors who designed that building. They designed in such a way," the engineers say, "that it cuts the water, and therefore there is no force for the water to wash away. A marvellous construction—and yet we don't know the materials in it. We know it is built with local resources. Some people say it may be horse hair, guinea grass...!"

It was this perspective of self-reliance which he brought to the role of the university in the national crisis of literacy. Beckford says:

> The battle for eradicating functional literacy, in our view, is so urgent that consideration should be given to closing the university for one academic year, and diverting student and staff activity to a national campaign.... In this connection, the urban to rural (and vice versa) movement would benefit the student-teacher whose knowledge of Jamaica's natural environment would be enhanced immeasurably....

The context in which knowledge is produced, acquired, and distributed has a decisive influence on the content and practice of such knowledge; and consequently, this context gives a certain shape to the ways in which we see and feel what we know. I work from the assumption that a mode of perception is not autonomous. It evolves and matures within a specific context, and its function reflects the context from which it is inseparable. Everyone bears witness to his or her own experience and is therefore engaged in the process of knowledge production, even when such knowledge is discovered to be in error. And knowledge is never passive. It is always intended to be put in the service of some specific intention. It may serve to protect and stabilize the dominant values of a particular context of social relations, or it may serve to subvert and transcend those values. But whatever course it takes, the result always carries the signature of a context. Knowledge is therefore social in character. Critical theory and practice must therefore be seen as forms of social enquiry: tools of analysis and exposition which seek to identify, isolate, and define the various components of a particular context. It may be a matter of fate where an existence first becomes aware of itself and its environment, or when and in what manner it is extinguished; but to be alive is to be in a process of enquiring how and to what purpose this existence may survive and reproduce itself. Even prayer, which assumes a history beyond time, is a form of enquiry. For the atheist, among the most religious of humans, prayer becomes a dialogue of defiance against the disabling charity of a divine transcendence.

The Practice of Literature is Rooted in these Questions

Literature, Freedom, and the Imagination

On the way to the tonelle in the novel *Season of Adventure*, the drummers, Crim and Powell, are trying to work their way through the contradictions with which the new Independence confronts them:

"So I put it to you as one man to a next."

"Who say I's a man?" And Crim's voice meant what he had asked.

"Is you self say so."

"When?"

"The very day you born."

"But I couldn't make a note with words that day," Crim argued.

"Is words make a note with you," said Powell, "like how you beat your drum till it shape a tune, words beat your brain till it language your tongue."

"Is what that got to do with man?"

"Every everything. Till then you ain't nothin' but a beast."

"Some beasts does talk."

"But talk aint nothin' till it ask," said Powell. "Man is a question the beast ask itself."

"All right, I's a man."

Or in a later contention over the nature and content of freedom: "I say it was a real freedom happen when the tourist army went away," Crim said.

"It look a real freedom they give San Cristobal." "It don't have that kind o' givin'," said Powell, trying to restrain his anger. "Is wrong to say that, 'cause free is free an' it don't have no givin'. Free is how you is from the start, an' when it look different you got to move, just move, an' when you movin' say that is a natural freedom make you move. You can't move to freedom, Crim, 'cause freedom is what you is, an' where you start, an' where you always got to stand.... If ever I give you freedom, Crim, then all your future is mine, 'cause whatever you do in freedom name is what I make happen. Seein' that way is a blindness from the start."

In *The Pleasures of Exile*, I had tried to construct a rereading of *The Tempest* that would reveal the problem of learning as a treacherous form of giving in any colonial encounter. Education, meaning the possession of the Word—which was in the beginning or not at all—is the tool Prospero had tried on the irredeemable nature of his savage and deformed slave Caliban. We are brought to the heart of the matter by the cantankerous assertion, spoken by Miranda, but obviously on the thought and vocabulary of her father:

MIRANDA: Abhorred slave,
        Which any print of goodness will
        not take,

> Being capable of all ill! I pitied thee,
> Took pains to make thee speak, taught thee each hour
> One thing or the other: when thou didst not, savage,
> Know thine own meaning, but wouldst gabble like
> A thing most brutish, I endow'd thy purposes
> With words that made them known. But thy vile race,
> Though thou didst learn, had that in't which good natures
> Could not abide to be with; therefore wast thou
> Deservedly confin'd into this rock,
> Who hadst deserve more than a prison.

Caliban is the occasion for establishing a mode and continuity of thought that would exercise across many centuries an immense and toxic influence on the architecture of knowledge which came to be known as the humanities. This perception of a "vile race/which good natures could not abide to be with," and which some of the finest minds of western culture could not wholly escape since history had bestowed on them a vertical location from which they could select and define whatever they thought worthy of serious scholarly attention.

It is interesting here to contrast the ways of seeing the same conjuncture of events by two great scholars who inherited that great divide initiated by the concept and device of race. In his remarkable history of the 20th century, *The Age of Extremes*, Eric Hobsbawm writes:

> Peace meant before 1914. In 1914 there had been no major war for a century, that is to say a war in which all, or even a majority of major powers, had been involved.... Between 1815 and 1914 no major power fought another outside its immediate region, although aggressive expeditions of imperial or would-be imperial powers against overseas enemies were, of course, common....

The tone and texture of language here perplexes the African-American scholar and writer, W. E. B. Du Bois, who reflects on the same events in his book, *The World and Africa*. Major war, for Hobsbawm, is confined to war in which "major powers had been involved"; and the destruction of alien civilizations is comfortably defined, "of course, [by] aggressive expeditions of imperial powers against weaker oversees enemies." The contrast is startling when we engage the full text of Du Bois's bewilderment about the peace movement of the 19th century:

> The paradox of the peace movement of the nineteenth century is a baffling comment on European

civilization. There was not a single year during the nineteenth century when the world was not at war. Chiefly, but not entirely, these wars were waged to subjugate colonial peoples. They were carried on by Europeans, and at least one hundred and fifty separate wars can be counted during the heyday of the peace movement. What the peace movement really meant was peace in Europe and between Europeans, while for the conquest of the world and because of the suspicion which they held toward each other, every nation maintained a standing army....

The world wars were Europe's civil wars. They only became world wars because, according to an African proverb, "When the elephants fight the grass gets trampled." The world was Europe's grass.

A system which for two centuries or more has left the majority of human kind in a state of illiteracy, poverty, and disease cannot be accepted as a model for the free, creative realization of the human spirit; nor the private property—and which can be interpreted as the freedom of corporate capitalism to encircle and consume the globe.

Miranda's theme of a "vile race/which good natures could not abide to be with" would later mature into a body of theory, which the authority of the German philosopher Immanuel Kant confirms by arguing for the inseparable bond between anthropology and geography:

In hot countries, the human matures earlier in all ways, but does not reach the perfection of the temperate zones. Humanity exists in its greatest perfection in a white race. The yellow Indians have a smaller amount of talent. The Negroes are lower. . . . That which the sun implants in the skin of the Negro in Africa and thus that which is only accidental to him, must fall away in France and only the blackness will remain which is his by birth, and which he reproduces, and which alone can thus be used as a difference in class...."

The influence of these pronouncements on future dictionaries is traceable even to this day. Thus *Webster's Third New International Dictionary* ascribes to the term "black" the connotations: "outrageously wicked, a villain, dishonourable, indicating disgrace, connected with the Devil...." On the other hand, "white" carries such connotations as "free from blemish, moral stain or impunity, decent.... In a fair upright manner, a sterling man."

This ideology was planted here the very first day the Admiral set foot on these shores. And in the concrete scenario of Trinidad and Tobago and Guyana the question would arise: Where is home and when does it begin? In the publication *Enterprise of the Indies*, the Indo-Trinidadian historian Dr. Kusha Haraksingh draws attention to the predicament of the first generation of Indian indentured laborers whose contract carried the condition of return to India after five years. A choice had to be made, and it is Dr. Haraksingh's contention that this choice to stay carried a symbolic significance which was deliberately ignored or lost on those who were not Indian:

> The decision to stay was often coupled with a residential move away from plantation to "free" villages, which itself often involved the acquisition of title to property. This served as a major platform to belonging, an urge that soon become more evident in efforts to redesign the landscape. Thus the trees which were planted around emergent homesteads, including religious vegetation, constitute[s] a statement about belonging; so too did the temples and mosques which began to dot the landscape. And the rearing of animals which could not be abandoned; and the construction of ponds and tanks, and the diversion of watercourses; and the clearing of lands. When all this is put together it is hard to resist the conclusion that Indians had begun to think of Trinidad as their home long before general opinion in the country had awakened to that as a possibility.

And there is evidence in many of our narratives of that perception of the Indian as alien and other, a problem to be contained after the departure of the imperial power. This has been a major part of the thought and feeling of West Indians of African descent, and a particularly stubborn conviction among the black middle classes of Trinidad and Guyana. Indian achievement in politics or business has been regarded as an example of an Indian strategy for conquest; and even where such achievement did not exist, there could still be heard the satirical assault on those Indians who appeared to identify too readily with a creolizing process. The calypsos between 1946 and the 1960s are the authentic examples of this.

But I believe that labor and the social relations experienced in the process of labor constitute the foundations of culture. It is through work that men and women make nature a part of their own history. The way we see, the way we hear, our nurtured sense of touch and smell, the whole complex of feelings which we call sensibility, is influenced by the particular features of the landscape that has been humanized by our work; so there can be no history of Trinidad or Guyana that is not also a history of the humanization of those landscapes by African and Indian forces of labor.

This is at once the identity and the conflict of interests that engaged the deepest feeling of those indentured workers inscribing their signatures on a landscape that will be converted into home and also the bitter taste of loss that the emancipated African experiences as he sees the same land become the symbol of his dispossession.

How to reconcile these contradictions with the past is for us, in these circumstances, not just an exercise in memory in the retrieval of some rationale of consolation for our labor. The past became a weapon that ethnicity summoned as evidence of group solidarity. Politics would become an expression of ethnic grievance made rational and just by any evidence the past could sanction.

And here was the burden of commitment that Walter Rodney assumed.

Conclusion

Walter Rodney as political activist and historian had sought to show that those Indians in the category of indentured labor had always waged heroic struggle against that condition (31 strikes in 1886, and 42 in 1888). This investment of labor and resistance had made them partners with their African brothers and sisters in a struggle to liberate a people and a region from the imperial encirclement of poverty, illiteracy, and self-contempt.

His scholarship sought to help dismantle a tradition that, before and after Independence, has used the device of race to obscure and sabotage the fundamental unity that married the destinies of Indian and African workers through their common experience of labor. A democratic future rested, above everything else, on the recognition of that historical fact, and the means whereby this could be absorbed and experienced as the most important truth of their daily lives, the characteristic features of all their social relations. Difference in cultural heritage is not an objective obstacle to such an achievement. Indeed, this cultural difference can only be accepted, respected, and cherished after the artificial conflict of race had been abolished by that unifying force which derives from their common experience of labor. It was this possibility that alarmed Rodney's executioners.

The colonization of the female by an arbitrary division of labor would in time give rise to a crusade in sexual politics which has become a major challenge to all established orthodoxy in the contemporary Caribbean, and the patriarchal character of Caribbean literature has been immensely enriched by the range and quality of women's writing. It's almost a certainty that one of the most fertile areas of its expansion will be occupied by what, previously and by traditional stereotype, was the most dormant of all voices: the voice of the Indo-Caribbean woman. Less than half a century of access to the school and the swift migration from barrack room and cane patch into the professional citadels of the nations' workplaces have now broken forever that curtain of silence and submission that we were made to believe was her chosen location. In the *Trinidad Express* special "Indian Arrival Supplement" of May 1992, Sita Bridgemohan offers this poignant statement of her claims on the Trinidad landscape: "My forefathers came from India to work in the canefields. They were Hindus. With sweat, tears, hard work and courage, they created a life in a different land, a land in which I was born. By right of birth, I have a place in this land and don't have to fight for it."

The concepts of race, nation, and ethnicity constitute a family of constructs of largely European origins, which served to influence the attitudes we should adopt to any encounter with difference. European racism was a form of ethnic nationalism that invested the color line with a power of definition that neither Asian nor African could have escaped.

Difference in religion and difference in modes of cultural affirmation now require a new agenda of perspectives, a wholly new way of looking at the concept of nation, of finding a way to immunize sense and sensibility against the virus of ethnic nationalism (for the culture of an ethnic group is no more than the set of rules into which parents belonging to that ethnic group are pressured to socialize their children) and to educate feeling to respect the autonomy of the Other's difference, to negotiate the cultural spaces that are the legitimate claim of the Other, and to work toward an environment which could manage stability as a state of creative conflict. The challenge of diversity and the peculiar nature of our own diasporic adventure could be made a fertilizing soil and the crusading theme of political discourse. Indeed, this diversity has been an abundant blessing for cultural workers in all the arts in the Caribbean: Creative conflict is the dynamic which drives the Caribbean imagination.

In his Nobel Prize speech (1992), Derek Walcott reveals the paradox and the utopian character of a vision which keeps our faith alive:

> Break a vase, and the love that reassembles the fragments is stronger than that love which took its symmetry for granted when it was whole. The glue that fits the pieces is the sealing of its original shape. It is such a love that reassembles our African and Asiatic fragments, the cracked heirlooms whose restoration shows its white scars. This gathering of broken pieces is the care and pain of the Antilles, and if the pieces are disparate, ill-fitting, they contain more pain than their original sculpture, those icons and sacred vessels taken for granted in their ancestral places. Antillean art is this restoration of our shattered histories, our shards of vocabulary, our archipelago becoming a synonym for pieces broken off from the original continent.

If language was a major instrument of Empire, it

is the very flexible and varying ranges of language, the subtle and explicit manipulations of native rhythms of speech, that have won our writers a very special attention. If the metropole directed what is standard and required by the cultural establishment, it is at the periphery of colony or neo-colony that the imagination resists, destabilizes, and transforms the status of the word in action. This is a mark of cultural sovereignty—the free definition and articulation of the collective self, whatever the rigor of external constraints.

Notes

[1] Lecture delivered by George Lamming at the conference in his honor, hosted by the Centre for Caribbean Thought, University of the West Indies, Jamaica, 2003. Lamming prefaced the original lecture with the following:

I HAVE ALREADY made it known that I have had a long and very joyful association with Jamaica; and although some of the delights of previous visits may recur, it is most unlikely that the special honor and resonance of this occasion will happen again. I thank you for the generosity of attention and appreciation that you have bestowed on me.

With your permission, I would like to share this moment and offer my address as a tribute to two great friends who have passed away. I first came to Jamaica at the invitation of John and Dorothy Figueroa to spend Christmas 1955 and was made a member of that family for all the years they lived here on this campus at Gibraltar Road. Dorothy was, as the tourist brochure says, "beyond imagination," but it is to John I owe, on behalf of a generation of writers, a debt for the role he played (as a professor of education) in preparing graduate students for the Diploma of Education and making the literature of the Caribbean a central obligation in their teaching responsibilities.

John Figueroa prepared the ground for professors Mervyn Morris and Kenneth Ramchand and Edward Baugh and the more rigorous scrutinisers of text who came later. And I am sure it was at his initiative, with the spontaneous support of Phillip Sherlock, that I would have come in 1967 as the writer-in-residence at Mona.

And the second loss that I have experienced, and more recently, was the passing of Tim Hector, who combined a magnificent and philosophical intelligence with the investigative skills of the journalist. These skills are aptly demonstrated in his lecture on West Indian cricket and Pan-Africanism.

John and Tim were very distant in social formation as well as ideological orientation: one Catholic, the other Marxist and humanist. But they shared two passions that would qualify them to be in paradise this afternoon. First is their belief that there was no game ever created that could rival the virtues and educated discipline of cricket, and second, whatever their ideological divide, they believed in and were committed to the Caribbean, however negligible it might appear to strangers, as a unique corner of the earth whose resources of intellect and imagination it was their business to nurture and defend. My talk rests on a dialogue with these important figures in Caribbean life.

Selected Bibliography

Beckford, George. "Sovereignty and Self-Reliance: The Economic Implications." In *Proceedings of a Regional Seminar on Caribbean Sovereignty. Mobilization for Development and Self-Reliance and the Tasks of Political Education*. Edited by Anthony Bogues. Kingston: People's National Party, 1985.

Carter, Martin. "A Free Community of Valid Persons: A Martin Carter Prose Sampler." *Kyk-Over-Al* 44 (May 1993).

Du Bois, W. E. B. *The World and Africa*. New York: International Publishers, 1965.

Goveia, Elsa. *Slave Society in the British West Indies to the end of the eighteenth century*. New Haven: Yale University Press, 1965.

Hobsbawm, Eric. *The Age of Extremes: A History of the World, 1914-1991*. New York: Vintage Books, 1996.

Manley, Michael. "Aspects of a Caribbean Development Strategy." In *Proceedings of a Regional Seminar on Caribbean Sovereignty: Mobilization for Development and Self-Reliance and the Tasks of Political Education*. Edited by Anthony Bogues. Kingston: People's National Party, 1985.

Marti, Jose. *Selected Writings*. London: Penguin, 2002.

Nettleford, Rex, ed. *Manley and the New Jamaica*. London: Longman, 1971.

Nurse, Lawrence. "Organized Labour in the Commonwealth Caribbean." In *A Caribbean Reader on Development*. Edited by Judith Wedderburn. Kingston: FES, 1986.

Rodney, Walter. *A History of the Guyanese Working People, 1881-1905*. Baltimore: Johns Hopkins University Press, 1981.

Shakespeare, William. *The Tempest*. London: Methuen & Company Ltd., 1954.

Williams, Eric. *Education of the Negro in the British West Indies*. Rpt. New York: A & B Books, 1994.

2

LANGUAGE AND THE POLITICS OF ETHNICITY[1]

The title of these reflections, "Language and the Politics of Ethnicity," is a title which would be described in critical theory as a site of contention. I would like in a way to diffuse the potential for contention by beginning with two voices separated by generations: that is, voices that are in a way echoing the same kind of interior journey of discovery.

The first is a voice from Guyana, Mahadai Das, "If I came to India":

> If I came to India
> shall I be on a broken pilgrimage
> to Mahatma?
> Resigned or rebellious
> at streetcorner hunger
> shall I wear a penitence, a saffron
> robe, wooden beads of my days
> cast about my breast?
> Shall I be Methuselah
> in my tradition, a foreign vine
> grafted to the Deccan Peninsula?
> Shall I find
> the poet naked in the mountain?
> Shall I discover philosophy
> in mountain-caves where

Everest reigns?
Near the Tibetan border
where monks levitate, is
the secret of Being written
on a parched leaf?
If I come
will I find my Self.[2]

The second is "My Last Name" from the Cuban Nicolás Guillén:

Well then, I ask you now:
Don't you see these drums in my eyes?
Don't you see these drums, tightened and
beaten with two dried-up tears
Don't I have, perhaps,
a nocturnal grandfather
with a great black scar
(darker still than his skin)
a great scar made by a whip?
Have I not, then,
a grandfather who's Mandingo, Dahoman,
Congolese?
What is his name? Oh, yes, give me his name!
Andrés? Francisco? Amable?
How do you say Andrés in Congolese?
How have you always said
Francisco in Dahoman?
In Mandingo, how do you say Amable?
No? Were they, then, other names?
The last name then!

> Do you know my other last name, the one that comes
> to me from that enormous land, the captured,
> bloody last name, that came across the sea
> in chains, which came in chains across the sea.[3]

In any consideration of the role of language in the politics of ethnicity of Diaspora cultures, it is always prudent to bear in mind the context or location from which you speak. It is context that gives meaning to every question you ask. "How many children do you have?" may appear to be a simple enough question. But it is context and location that will soon reveal its complexity. For an example of the importance of context, I must take you back to a visit I made to Kenya in the mid-1970s. I had spent a day in the village of Limuru, at the home of the very distinguished novelist, Ngugi wa Thiong'o. There was a big family and much jubilation all around. In a very relaxed way I asked him, "How many children do you have?" He asked me in turn whether I would like to have another drink. I said, "Yes, of course," accepted the drink, and repeated my question, "How many children...?" And he said, "As we were saying before...." This abrupt detour made it clear there was not going to be an answer to my question. A day later I was talking to a mutual friend and reported this episode. I was told, "Oh, but no, no, no, no. That question wouldn't be answered. Among the Kikuyu, you never count offspring; to do so is to invite calamity." And now, decades later, it makes me think how extraordinary are the multiple frontiers of behavior we have to explore and negotiate to find ways of entering with courtesy into each other's world.

Language is essentially a very political tool, and the term political is used here to define the dynamics of a people's cultural evolution, the way we organize our social lives together, and the power relations that this involves. It is in the context of our political culture that we recognize the decisive authority of power in the creation of words and in the intentional construction of the sentence. I want to give you two examples to illustrate a certain historical continuity in two distinct geographical locations.

In the early 1970s, I was giving some lectures to what was then the Extra-Mural Department of the University of the West Indies. It was the same afternoon of my arrival in Antigua that my host and I ran into the minister of education whom I was meeting for the first time. When he heard that I was going to speak on the evolution of Caribbean literature, his response was immediate and uncompromising: "Don' bring no broken English in my school please," he said, completed the handshake, and continued on his business. The university representative appeared embarrassed, but it was, for me, a very fruitful example of the contradictions at work in the consciousness of this honorable citizen. His reproach was itself a fine example of breaking up the English language which he had asked to be left unimpaired.

In 1976, an even more complex situation arose on the island of St. Lucia, where English is the official language of instruction. However, the island's long experience of French rule had bestowed on St. Lucia the gift of another tongue so that the entire population, irrespective of social background, is born into an oral tradition of Kwéyòl, which has the pervasive character of a national language. Everybody speaks it, but it is not accorded the authority of English, which is the language of government and the official exchange required by state institutions.

The situation I am referring to here involved an elected member of the country's parliament who rose and gave the speaker warning that he was going to address the parliament in Creole (Kwéyòl). The speaker said he could not because the existing constitution did not allow it. When the member persisted, the speaker threatened him with expulsion from the Chamber. The threat was made in Creole, purely as a matter of emphasis and intention.

The contradiction is not strictly speaking about language—it is about Power; it is about the politics of cultural subjugation and the transitional period of resistance to that hierarchical authority which makes a clear distinction between the language of negotiation (that is government, school, church, and so on) and language in action (the language of the marketplace, the school yard, the playing field)—between let us say state language and street or people's language. The minister of education may have had good reason to be worried, for the orthodoxies of language he represented were being transformed into bridges through the subversive intervention of our novelists and poets, who had narrowed the distance between what was called Standard English and the variety of nonstandard forms, which are now the occasion of much academic critical scrutiny.

Language was a major instrument in the creation of Empire. There is remarkable evidence from some 19th-century diaries that Empire has also been a metaphor of racial diversity and cultural miscegenation that challenges the imagination to discover its true location. The Antigua minister of education would have found a sympathetic missionary witness in Lady Maria Nugent, whose journal was written between 1801 and 1805 and with the authority and privilege of the wife of the governor of Jamaica. She has a very fine sense of the relation of language to power, and laments the influence of the black tongue on the English ladies around her:

The Creole language is not confined to the negroes. Many of the ladies, who have not been educated in England, speak a sort of broken English, with an indolent drawling out of their words, that is very tiresome if not disgusting. I stood next to a lady one night, near a window, and, by way of saying something, remarked that the air was much cooler than usual; to which she answered, "Yes, ma-am, *him rail-ly too fra-ish.*"[4]

But if it is the sound, indolent, and tedious drawling which disturbed Lady Nugent, the Reverend William Jones, who was on that island during the same period, is struck by a more dangerous tendency: the way language may be experienced as a mode of thinking, receiving, and articulating experience:

> I have heard it observed as a fault of the white inhabitants, that instead of correcting the crude speech of the Negroes and better informing them, they descend so low as to join in their gibberish and by insensible degrees almost acquire the same habit of thinking and speaking.[5]

We must ask, "Is this mockery or is it the initial stages in the process of transculturation?" Journeys of conquest, initiated by an interior thirst for expansion, order, and settlement, give way to involuntary migration and the conflicting claims of different groups to equal partnership in new homelands. Our context and location, which is the Caribbean, is perhaps a unique enclosure for identifying these histories of dominance and transculturation. The narratives recur of Europe imposing its will on the pastoral landscapes of Aboriginal peoples whose world collapses and fragments and then dissolves before new waves of Africans in bondage and rebellion. Subsequently came the arrival of East Indians indentured to sugar plantations, whose lives alternated between jail and hospital, strike and sickouts, and who were architects of resistance as were their African predecessors.

In order to prepare ourselves for conflict (and conflict must be accepted as a norm and not a distortion), we must remind ourselves of the unique character of this movement of peoples into this archipelago and remember that in this struggle of finding self through language and discovering language through self, we have a situation in which there are many contestants making rival claims on our attention. There is not only an African diaspora, there is also an Indian and wider Asian diaspora, and this confluence generates a tense creative challenge in the demands for democratic claims on the landscape. It is from this turmoil of diverse human encounters that Lady Nugent's term *Creole* acquires a very special resonance and a resonance for us that would have been beyond her imagination. For it is a word I know which subverts traditional orthodoxies of inheritance and at the same time offers itself as a stabilizing constraint on the fragmenting tendencies inherent in a plural society.

To avoid too great a conflict about the different applications of the term "creole," I am going to settle for a single derivation in the Spanish *criar*, which means in the Caribbean context to nourish, to nurse, to bring forth, to be the evolving product of, and to indigenize. We choose that route/root because it opens the possibility of an *authentic civic nationalism* that would embrace every self-defined ethnic type. Time and the political economy of the landscape in the form of the plantation allowed no one to be exempt from the inexorable process of creolization. There are those who claim European ancestry, but who were made, shaped, and seeded by the cultural forces of the archipelago, and whose interaction with others have made them a distinct breed from the stock from whom they have descended. Fernando Ortiz and the discovery of Cubanidad is a fine example.

Moreover, the relations of intimacy, voluntary or otherwise, which diagnosed plantation society in the Caribbean did not allow for any reliable claim to any form of ancestral purity. Creole is the name of their anatomy. The sons and daughters of Indian indentured labor arriving in the third decade of the 19th century may argue a stronger case for ancestral heritage than their African predecessors, but this proximity in time to the ancestral homeland does not erase or obscure their sense of belonging to the creolized world of Trinidad or Guyana.

The Indian discomfort with the term creole (and it is a word that arouses a certain antagonism) cannot be a denial of the process of creolization, although it may be a correct rejection of the cultural dominance that power conferred on one particular ethnic group. In his essay, "Asian Identity and Culture in the Caribbean," Brinsley Samaroo raises the very vexatious question:

> When therefore the Indo-Caribbean person is being constantly told that he must subscribe to the larger ill-defined something that is Creole culture, we must ask the more relevant question, namely, what is there in that culture that is superior to what orientalism offers?[6]

Orientalism is a European concept unacceptable to the Indo-Caribbean and therefore an awkward alternative with which to challenge. But it is this use of orientalism that brings us to the heart of the question. It was the European dominant mode of thought which gave a decisive shape and content to the entire Colonial experience, and the Africans' longer and more intimate association with this mode of thought made creolization appear to be a more natural and affirming inheritance than his Indian equivalent could accept. Creolization is not a static condition, but an open-ended process of collective self-definition and deepening indigenization. It cannot be thought of as the final and irreversible project.

The African scholar Ali Mazrui, in his essay "Terminological Ethnocentrism," has made a bold and uncomfortable observation:

> The West has invented an entire vocabulary which has landed us with unprecedented ways of thinking about our planet, a planet which we all share. This little continent called Europe went around naming this, that and the other, and it stuck. And we cannot think of the world in terms other than those of words they bequeathed to us.[7]

Against all reason, we go on using terms like *Far East* and *Near East* without wondering, far from where, near where, because we know the answer is Europe. And it is the consequence of this Eurocentric triumph that much of the world, including the Caribbean, is engaged in resisting and wherever possible neutralizing. Globalization is not new. It is an old European adventure that has evolved with miraculous virulence into a Euro-American nightmare for the poor, small, and powerless.

But it may also be helpful to remind ourselves that

we distort reality if we encourage thinking about Africans and Indians in uniform and monolithic terms. Controversy about self-definition prevails not only between different groups but also between different layers of the same group. There is a relevant and very touching autobiographic passage form Cheddi Jagan's *The West on Trial* (1966). He is discussing the emotional shock experienced during his transition from rural to urban living as a school boy of about twelve and a boarder in Georgetown:

> To compensate ... for the small amount of money my father paid for my board and lodging, I had to do many chores such as washing the elder's car, carrying his lunch on my bicycle, going to market and cutting grass for his goats. I particularly resented the latter. Cutting and fetching grass in the country was one thing; but doing so in Georgetown as a Queen's College student was quite another. Georgetown middle-class snobbery had so influenced me that I soon found some pretext to persuade my father to find me other lodgings.[8]

Dr. Jagan escaped from the indignities of cutting and fetching grass under the glare of Georgetown, but something no less painful was to follow and he continues:

> The new family with whom I stayed being of the Kshatriya caste. One of the daughters had married

a Brahmin and had three sons and one daughter.... Two things particularly irked me about my position in this household: firstly, I was singled out to go occasionally to the market; secondly, I had to sleep on the floor, although there was an empty room with a vacant bed. Apparently this was for reasons of status, based on caste — my family was Kurmi, lower in status than a Kshatriya or a Brahmin. Until then, ... I had heard my mother occasionally mention caste, I had never really encountered it....[9]

Caribbean literature will provide us with the most vivid description of the school as an institution whose most critical function or dysfunction was to initiate and make permanent the existing layers of social stratification. Deschooling the mind from this early catastrophe is an agonizing task. C. L. R. James spent much of a long life negotiating a complete divorce from Queen's Royal College, and he was to say, "It was only long years after that I understood the limitation on spirit, vision and self-respect which was imposed upon us."[10]

This phenomenon of social distance, of class, is common to all ethnic categories and is a very decisive influence in the process of cultural formation. A large Indian agricultural proletariat in Trinidad or Guyana would not be unaware of the difference in the material interests that distance them from the modernizing consumerist lifestyle of their own professional and entrepreneurial elites. Nor is the African creole working class any less aware of this divide among Afro-Trinidadians. But individuals responding to the imagined threat of group pressure are very vulnerable to the most vulgar and opportunistic appeals which warn them about probable destruction by the Other. And when the political goal is not just about securing minority civil rights, but actually acquiring the instruments of power for the regulation of the total society, racial and ethnic demagogy on either side makes sure of its advantages, even when the fundamental issue is not objectively about Race but Power.

In her novel, *Sastra*, Lakshmi Persaud engages the character Dr. Capildeo in a discourse on this organic connection between the construct of race and the exercise of power. After a disastrous fire, thought to be arson set by Afro-Trinidad rivals, Dr. Capildeo offers this explanation:

> ... we must come to terms with the fact that whichever group is in power, once it has a majority, it will keep power and stay there until the resurrection, because, no matter how corrupt they are, what a mess they make of things, year in year out, all the time, at the back of their minds, they know they have a trump card—the strong tribal card—primeval, instinctive. They only have to play it on that deep gut prejudice, that preference for ourselves when under threat.[11]

There are numerous examples in our literature of hostility between individuals that derive from these toxic sources of power that manipulate the original neutral difference between characters: the innocent malice, for example, of Mazie directed at Philomen in James's *Minty Alley* and the censoring of Pariag's inclusion and participation by the yard in Earl Lovelace's *The Dragon Can't Dance*. The strategy of ensuring allegiance by dramatizing the menace of the Indian was most effectively used by the old colonial power, and it has often been called into service by both African and Indian political leadership in the new independent countries. It has been a major obstacle to the realization of an *authentic civic nationalism* that will embrace and recreolize all ethnic types in Caribbean society.

It was my first experience, really, of Guyana when I discovered the theme for *Of Age and Innocence* (1958). In this novel I tried to explore a reflection and what were the inherent possibilities that existed in what was then the People's Progressive Party (PPP) in Guyana. Something quite extraordinary happened in Guyana in the early 1950s. What was new, and I think without precedent, was the forging of two separate armies of labor—African and Indian—into a single political force and the creation of a consciousness born of that collaboration which led these armies of labor to understand that they were the foundation on which the social order rested. It was no doubt this newly-forged consciousness, combined with their numerical superiority and the morality of their purpose, that equipped them to challenge and ultimately seek to dismantle the colonial authority's structure of rule in what was then British Guyana.

In the early 1950s, the PPP in Guyana created an environment and a sense of possibilities and expectations that affected in one way or another every section of the society. It set the agenda of intellectual discourse that influenced the mood and themes of creative expression. This was the soil from which the early and strongest poems of the Guyanese Martin Carter would blossom. This was the soil that nourished Gordon Rohlehr and Walter Rodney, and neither of them succumbed to the virus of ethnocentricity. But the dream of Martin Carter suffered a traumatic collapse from which, in my view, the peoples of Guyana have never quite recovered.

I am aware of the external forces that were hostile to this dream, the manipulative power of those forces able to intervene and erode what was in the making. However, I do not think we can settle for this as a sole explanation of the collapse of that radical movement. A fundamental part of the weakness of that historical moment resulted from the party leadership assuming a human solidarity that had not yet been consolidated. This attribute of human solidarity is not a given; this attribute of human solidarity does not arise by chance or miracle. It has to be learned; it has to be nurtured; it has to be cultivated. This requires a kind of educational work, a kind of indoctrination, a reciprocal sharing of cultural histories, which has never been at the center of our political agendas in the Caribbean.

Perhaps there was not time enough; perhaps it was a misfortune that the PPP came to power when it did in Guyana in 1953. Perhaps a period of opposition without consuming their energies in the emergencies of administration might have allowed for that fundamental groundwork in political education and cultural dialogue. This recent consciousness of possibilities among the ranks of labor would have given a new dimension and a most substantial content. But tolerance was the adjustment they made in the struggle, and tolerance is a fragile bond. When the leadership broke, the armies turned on each other with a tribal and atavistic fury. We ourselves had fertilized the ground for the enemy to plant further mischief. I think it is a profound illusion and a tragic error to transfer this act of self-mutilation to a foreign conscience we call Imperialist. There are certain defeats for which we must be prepared to take full responsibility.

In Barbados, the concept of race was articulated most effectively through the division of labor. (Agricultural labor was very exclusively black, bank clerks exclusively white.) We've witnessed the reversal of roles in the administration of the country. Now the executive branch of the state—that is the government, the judiciary, and the upper layers of the civil service—are almost entirely black. There is no traditional anxiety of an Indian threat. But the loss or conceding of political power by white Barbados has alerted us to a novel and challenging grievance from the literate voices of that social entity. In the *Trinidad and Tobago Review* publication *Enterprise of the Indies*, the journalist Robert Goddard, who is a member of a very powerful white Barbadian merchant family, makes a charge of Afrocentrism and its debilitating effect on the prospect of regional coherence:

> Black nationalism in the region is predicated on the idea that the West Indies is culturally black, and by inescapable implication, racially black as well. To be black is to be authentically Caribbean. To be non-black is to be an intruder.... Many white West Indians can relate to situations where they have disappointed non-West Indians by appearing in the flesh wearing a white skin, as it were, after their accent had led their listeners to assume they must be black on the telephone.[12]

I offer this as an example of the truth we are very reluctant to accept: that race and ethnicity are socially constructed categories. Mr. Goddard's voice on the telephone is ethnically black. On appearance, his skin reveals him to be racially white. He wears both categories: same citizen, two ways of being, located in the civic frame of reference. We have given these categories the power to generate antagonisms that affect our sectional and communal interest at the expense and even the sacrifice of a *liberating civic nationalism*.

The question arises: Where is home, and when does it begin? In this same publication, *Enterprise of the Indies*, the Indo-Trinidad historian, Kusha Haraksingh, in a remarkable contribution, draws attention to the predicament of the first generation of the Indian indentured laborers whose contract carried the condition of return to India after five years. A choice had to be made, and it is Haraksingh's contention that this choice to stay carried a symbolic significance that was deliberately ignored or lost on those who were not Indian:

> The decision to stay was often coupled with a residential move away from plantations to "free" villages, which itself often involved the acquisition of title to property. This served as a major platform for belonging; an urge that soon become more evident

in efforts to redesign the landscape. Thus, the trees which were planted around emergent homesteads, including religious vegetation, constituted a statement about belonging; so too did the temples and mosques which began to dot the landscape. And the rearing of animals which could not be abandoned; and the construction of ponds and tanks; and the diversion of watercourses; and the clearing of lands. When all this is put together, it is hard to resist the conclusion that Indians had begun to think of Trinidad as their home long before general opinion in the country had awakened to that possibility.[13]

There is abundant evidence in many of our narratives of that perception of the Indian as alien and other, a problem to be contained after the departure of the imperial Power. This has been a major part of the thought and feeling of many citizens of African descent and a particularly stubborn conviction among the black middle classes of Trinidad and Guyana. Indian achievement in politics or business has been regarded as an example of an Indian strategy for conquest; and even where such achievement did not exist, there could still be heard the satirical assault on those Indians who appeared to identify too readily with a creolizing process, Gordon Rohlehr has been very helpful here in his inventory of calypsos, and if you check the calypsos between 1946 and the 1960s, these are authentic examples of what we are saying:

> What's wrong with these Indian people?
> As though their intention is for trouble.
> Long ago you'd meet an Indian boy by the road
> With his capra waiting to tote your load
> But I notice there is no Indian again
> Since the women and them taking Creole name.
> Long ago was Sumintra, Ramaliwia,
> Bullbasia and Oosankalia
> But now is Emily, Jean and Dinah
> And Doris and Dorothy....[14]

And the mischievous mocking of Ramjohn's struggle for literacy:

> Ramjohn taking lessons daily
> From a high school up in Laventille
> The first day's lesson was dictation
> And a little punctuation
> After class he come home hungry to death
> His wife eh cook Ramjohn start to fret
> Whole day you sit down on you big fat comma
> And you eh cook nothing up
> But ah go put this hyphen in you semi-colon
> And bust your full stop and stop....[15]

If there is something blasphemous or heretical in this kind of representation, it becomes less so when this drama is seen from a different perspective.

The significance of Indians making a home may now be weighed against the African's rebellious feeling that a home has been stolen. In his very remarkable novel *Salt* (1996), Earl Lovelace traces through four or five generations, the history of this feeling, which the character Jo-Jo records. He has been a rebel and a runaway who lost an ear as punishment, but with rumors of emancipation, he sends petitions to Her Majesty through her Secretary of State for Colonial Development and his argument runs like this:

> As a result of the circumstances of our enslavement Your Memorialists have no other option now but to make this island their home since it is the place that many of them have been born into and it is the place that their labour has gone to build.[16]

The appeal is ignored, and we witness the bewilderment when he encounters for the first time a presence of which he had vaguely heard:

> One morning Jo-Jo was out in the yard, just about to go to the estate, when he heard the sound of cutlassing from the land nearby. He stopped for a moment in something between alarm and vexation. Grasping his own cutlass, Jo-Jo moved to the sound and found himself looking at one of the Indian men cutting the bush. His anger grew even more. These people bold. They come and take over the work and prevent the Governor from dealing with his petition, now, here is one of them squatting on the government land.

"Hey," Jo-Jo called out, "what is it you doing? You don't see people living here? How you come in here just so and don't tell nobody nothing?"

The Indian man looked at him in sober outrage and when he spoke he so choked up that his voice came out almost apologetic. "This land is my own."

"Your own?"

"Is because of my contract, I not going back to India."

"Your contract? You have contract? Who give you this contract?" Jo-Jo interrogating him as if he was Protector of Crown Lands.

"What happen," the Indian man ask him, "You working here?"

"Yes I working here," Jo-Jo answered.

"You working here and you don't know what a contract is? You don't have one? They didn't make one with you? How long you here?"

"Well for a fella who just come here, I find you asking a lotta question," Jo-Jo tell him. "I don't even know your name."

"I name Feroze. Look, I have my paper right here."

Jo-Jo took the paper. He looked at it. He handed it back to Feroze. He didn't say nothing.

"So, they didn't make a contract with you?" Feroze was uneasy.

"No, I ain't have none," Jo-Jo tell him, "I have no contract."

"How long you working here, man?"

"How long? Man, I thought I was asking the questions?"

"And I answering you. But you not bound to answer me? How long?"

Jo-Jo did not answer.

"Well maybe is because you from around here," Feroze said. "They don't have to pay passage for you. I from India. I from far across the sea. They have to pay plenty money for me to travel."

"Yes," Jo-Jo said. "Plenty money for me to travel."

"So where you from, pardner?"

"Pardner? Me? ... I from just across the sea there. From Africa."

And it's only then that Feroze caught on. You could see his mind working, "Why?" and before he could finish the question, Jo-Jo said, "Why I still here? I know you would ask that, I know it."

"Sorry," Feroze tell him, "I just come here to work."

"Don't worry to be sorry," Jo-Jo tell him, "I will tell you what I doing here."

"Really," Feroze said. "You don't have to tell me nothing, I just come to work this piece of land here."

"No, let me tell you," Jo-Jo tell him. "What I doing here is waiting." And he walked away.

"You know," he told Faustin, "they give these Indian people contract and land to work on these estates."

"It not their fault," Faustin tell him. "You should have squat on a piece of land yourself."

But Jo-Jo did not agree. It was clear to him that the Colony's treatment of the Indians had given him an even greater claim to reparation, but what was worrying, was his feeling that he had made an enemy of Feroze and the rest of Indian people.[17]

This fracture would remain unhealed, but it would also alert the imagination to the possibility of a novel kind of generosity. It is this possibility to which Derek Walcott refers in his 1992 Nobel speech:

> Break a vase, and the love that reassembles the fragments is stronger than that love which took its symmetry for granted when it was whole. The glue that fits the pieces is the sealing of its original shape. It is such a love that reassembles our African and Asiatic fragments, the cracked heirlooms whose restoration shows its white scars. This gathering of broken pieces is the care and pain of the Antilles, and if the pieces are disparate, ill-fitting, they contain more pain than the original sculpture, those icons and sacred vessels taken for granted in their ancestral places. Antillean art is this restoration of our shattered histories, our shards of vocabulary, our archipelago becoming a synonym for pieces broken off from the original continent.[18]

I believe that labor and the relations experienced in the process of labor constitute the foundation of all culture. It is through work that men and women make nature a part of their own history. The way we see, the way we hear, our nurtured sense of touch and smell, the whole complex of feelings which we call sensibility is influenced by the particular features of the landscape which has been humanized by our work. And so, there can be no history of Trinidad or Guyana that is not also the history of the humanization of those landscapes by African and Indian forces of labor.

This is at once the identity and the conflict of interests which engage the deepest feeling of those indentured workers inscribing their signatures on a landscape that would be converted into home, and also the bitter taste of loss, which the emancipated African Jo-Jo experiences as he sees land become a symbol of his dispossession. How to reconcile these contradictions was really the engagement of creative artists for its resolution. But the past was for us in these circumstances, not just an exercise in memory, and the retrieval of some ration of consolations for our labor, the past became a weapon which ethnicity summoned as evidence of group solidarity. Politics would become an expression of ethnic grievance made rational and just by any evidence which the Past could sanction. We were given warning of this sentiment when Jo-Jo, in spite of the undeserved card which the emancipation had played him, experiences a worry he would never have wished on anyone: "What was worrying him was his feeling that he had made an enemy of Feroze and the rest of the Indian people."[19]

The colonization of the female by an arbitrary division of labor would in time give rise to a crusade in sexual politics, which has become a major challenge to all established orthodoxy in the contemporary Caribbean. And the patriarchal character of Caribbean literature has been immensely enriched by the range and quality of women's writing. It is almost a certainty that one of the most fertile areas of its expansion would be occupied by what previously and by traditional stereotype was the most dormant of all voices, the voices of the Indo-Caribbean woman. Less than half a century of access to the school and with the swift migration from barrack room and cane patch to the professional citadels of the nation's workplace, these voices have now broken forever that curtain of silence and submission, which we were made to believe was their chosen location. In the Trinidad *Express*, in the Arrival supplement 1992, Sita Bridgemohan offers this poignant statement of her claims on the Trinidad landscape:

> My forefathers came from India to work in the canefields. They were Hindus. With sweat, tears,

hard work, and courage, they created a life in a different land, a land in which I was born. By right of birth, I have a place in this land and don't have to fight for it.

If African labor and the cultural dimensions of that labor constitute the first floor on which this Caribbean house was built, then the second floor and central pillar on which its creative survival depends is the total democratic participation of the Indo-Caribbean presence.

The concepts Race, Nation, and Ethnicity constitute a family of constructs of largely European origin, which served to influence the attitudes we should adopt to any encounter with difference. European racism was a form of ethnic nationalism that invested the color line with a power of definition which neither Asian nor African colonized could have escaped.

Difference in religion, difference in modes of cultural affirmation, require a new agenda of perspectives, a wholly new way of looking at the concept of nation, of finding a way to immunize sense and sensibility against the virus of ethnic nationalism (for the culture of an ethnic group is no more than the set of rules into which parents belonging to that ethnic group are pressured to socialize their children) in order to educate feeling to respect the autonomy of the Others' difference, to negotiate the cultural spaces that are the legitimate claim of the Other, and to work toward an environment that could manage stability as a state of creative conflict.

The challenge of diversity and the peculiar nature of our own diasporic adventure could be made a fertilizing soil and the crusading theme of political party discourse. Indeed, this diversity has been an abundant blessing for cultural workers in all the arts in the Caribbean: the novel, the visual arts, the syncretic splendor of our festivals. Creative conflict is the dynamic which drives the Caribbean imagination.

I have never been able to separate the creative imagination from the political culture in which it functions. And so, I will close with an extract from the American sociologist, the late C. Wright-Mills's *Power, Politics, and People*: "The independent artist and intellectual are among the few remaining personalities presumably equipped to resist and to fight the stereotyping and consequent death of genuinely living things. Fresh perception now involves the capacity to unmask and smash the stereotypes of vision and intellect with which modern communications *(that is modern systems of representations now)* swamp us. These worlds of mass-art and mass-thought are increasingly geared to the demands of" market politics. That is why it is in politics that intellectual solidarity and effort must be centred. "If the thinker does not relate himself *(or herself)* to the value of truth in political struggle, he *(or she)* cannot responsibly cope with the whole of live experience."[20]

And this has been the singular privilege and burden of my entire adult life, to help to create a civil environment that would teach the love and nurturing of genuine living things.

Notes

[1] Lecture sponsored by the Humanities department of the University of the West Indies, St. Augustine, Trinidad and Tobago, January 2004.
[2] Mahadai, "If I Came to India," 37.
[3] Guillén, "My Last Name," 75.
[4] Nugent, *Lady Nugent's Journal*, 98.
[5] Jones, *The Diary of the Reverend William Jones*.
[6] Samaroo, "Asian Identity and Culture in the Caribbean," 45.
[7] Kokole, *The Global African: A Portrait of Ali A. Mazrui*, 158-59.
[8] Jagan, *The West on Trial*, 22.
[9] Ibid.
[10] James, *Beyond a Boundary*, 38.
[11] Persaud, *Sastra*, 84.
[12] Goddard, "Last to Bat," 32-33.
[13] Haraksingh, "Indenture and Self Emancipation," 40.
[14] Mighty Killer, "Indian People with Creole Name," 498.
[15] The Mighty Skipper, "Punctuation."
[16] Lovelace, *Salt*, 181–82.
[17] Lovelace, *Salt*, 185–87.
[18] Walcott, *The Antilles: Fragments of Epic Memory*, 8-9.
[19] Lovelace, *Salt*, 187.
[20] Mills, *Power, Politics, and People*, 299.

Bibliography

Das, Mahadai. "If I Came to India." In *Enterprise of the Indies*. Edited by George Lamming. Port of Spain: Trinidad and Tobago Institute of the West Indies, 1999.

Goddard, Robert. "Last to Bat." In *Enterprise of the Indies*. Edited by George Lamming. Port of Spain: Trinidad and Tobago Institute of the West Indies, 1999.

Guillén, Nicolás. "My Last Name." *In Man-making Words.* Translated by Robert Márquez and David Arthur McMurray. Havana: Editorial de Arte y Literatura, 1973.

Haraksingh, Kusha. "Indenture and Self Emancipation." In *Enterprise of the Indies*. Edited by George Lamming. Port of Spain: Trinidad and Tobago Institute of the West Indies, 1999.

Jagan, Cheddi. *The West on Trial.* Berlin: Seven Seas Books, 1966.

James, C. L. R. *Beyond a Boundary.* London: Hutchinson, 1963.

Jones, William. *The Diary of the Reverend William Jones.* Edited by O. F. Christie. London: Brentano's, 1929.

Kokole, Omari H. *The Global African: A Portrait of Ali A. Mazrui.* Africa World Press, 1998.

Lovelace, Earl. *Salt*, London: Faber and Faber, 1996.

Mighty Killer. "Indian People with Creole Name" (1952). In *Calypso and Society in Pre-Independence Trinidad*. By Gordon Rohlehr. Port of Spain: Lexicon, 1990.

Mills, C. Wright. *Power, Politics, and People: The Collected Essays of C. Wright Mills.* London: Oxford University Press, 1967.

Nugent, Maria. *Lady Nugent's Journal.* Edited by Phillip Wright. Barbados, Jamaica, Trinidad, and Tobago: The University of the West Indies Press, 2002.

Persaud, Lakshmi. *Sastra.* Leeds: Peepal Tree Books, 1993.

Samaroo, Brinsely. "Asian Identity and Culture in the Caribbean." In *Enterprise of the Indies*. Edited by George Lamming. Port of Spain: Trinidad and Tobago Institute of the West Indies, 1999.

The Mighty Skipper. "Punctuation." In *Calypso Exposed*. San Francisco: Cook Records, 1961.

Walcott, Derek. *The Antilles: Fragments of Epic Memory.* New York: Farrar, Straus and Giroux, 1993.

About the Author

George Lamming is an illustrious Caribbean novelist and cultural critic from Barbados. His novels and volumes of essays and literary criticism offer insightful analyses on history, western philosophy, racism, colonization, education, literature and Caribbean independence. The Lamming titles include: *In the Castle of My Skin*, *Natives of My Person*, *Of Age and Innocence*, *Season of Adventure*, *The Emigrants*, *Water with Berries*, and *Coming, Coming Home: Conversations II – Western Education and the Caribbean Intellectual*. *Conversations II* has been translated into French and Spanish. The first of the Lamming "conversations" *Conversations, George Lamming: Essays, Addresses and Interviews 1953-1990* was published in 1992. Lamming also edited *Cannon Shot and Glass Beads: Modern Black Writing* and *Enterprise of the Indies*, and co-edited the Barbados and Guyana independence issues of *New World Quarterly*. Awards and honors include a fellow of the Institute of Jamaica, the Brachman Award from Yale University, the Casa de Las Américas Award, a Guggenheim, the Somerset Maugham Award, a Canadian Council Fellowship, a British Commonwealth Foundation grant, the Langston Hughes Award, and an honorary doctorate from the University of the West Indies and City University of New York. The University of the West Indies designated 2008 as the "Year of George Lamming" at its Cave Hill campus. George Lamming is a distinguished visiting professor at Brown University.